BIBLE STO

The Good Samaritan
and
The Boy Who Left Home

ILLUSTRATED BY STEPHANIE McFETRIDGE BRITT

THE GOOD SAMARITAN AND THE BOY WHO LEFT HOME
Copyright © 1998 Angus Hudson Ltd.
/Tim Dowley & Peter Wyart trading as
Three's Company

Text copyright © 1949 and 1998 Enid Blyton
Ltd. All rights reserved

The Enid Blyton Signature is a registered
Trademark™ of Enid Blyton Ltd., London

First published in 1998 by Candle Books,
England

Published in the United States of America
by Harvest House Publishers, Eugene,
Oregon 97402

ISBN 1-56507-992-2

Scripture quotes are taken from the Holy
Bible, New International Version®,
Copyright © 1973, 1978, 1984 by the
International Bible Society. Used by
permission of Zondervan Publishing House.
The "NIV" and "New International
Version" trademarks are registered in the
United States Patent and Trademark Office
by International Bible Society.

Designed and created by
Three's Company,
5 Dryden Street,
London WC2E 9NW

Illustrations by
Stephanie McFetridge Britt

Worldwide coedition organized and
produced by
Angus Hudson Ltd.,
Concorde House,
Grenville Place,
London NW7 3SA

For further information on Enid Blyton
please contact www.blyton.com

Printed in Singapore.

98 99 00 01 02/10 9 8 7 6 5 4 3 2 1

The Good Samaritan

This is a tale of great kindness. It is one of the best of all the tales that Jesus told. He was always preaching kindness and love, and in this story He tells us of a kind and good man.

Once upon a time there was a man who had to travel through the mountains along a lonely road that went from Jerusalem to Jericho.

As he went along, robbers saw him. They had their hiding-place among the rocks. They pounced upon the man and caught him.

He shouted for help. He struggled and tried to beat them off, but there were too many for him to fight. They hit the poor man again and then left him, carrying off his clothes as well as his money.

5

The man was too badly hurt to walk. He could only lie by the roadway, groaning in pain.

At last he heard the sound of feet. The wounded man lifted his head and saw to his joy that it was a priest of God who was coming by.

"Help!" he cried, feebly. "Help!"

The priest saw the man. He did not go to look at him. He crossed to the other side of the road and went on his way. The wounded man could hardly believe that anyone could be so cruel.

Then someone else came by. This time it was a Levite, a man often in the Holy Temple, who worshiped God and prayed to Him. He would surely help!

The Levite looked at the wounded man. He saw that he had hardly any clothes and that he had been robbed and wounded. But he did not help the man at all. He went calmly on his way and forgot all about the wounded traveler.

At last the man heard footsteps once more. He saw a man from Samaria—a Samaritan. The wounded man was disappointed.

"I have always heard that the Samaritans are mean and selfish," he thought. "Why, the priests and the Levites think themselves better than the Samaritans and would not even sleep in the same house with one of them. This Samaritan will not think of helping me."

The Samaritan suddenly saw the man lying by the roadside. He rode right up to him. He saw at a glance that the man was badly hurt and had been lying by the road for a long time.

"Poor fellow!" thought the Samaritan. "Robbers have set upon him and robbed him. They have beaten him cruelly. I must do something for him. What can I put on his wounds?"

Strapped on the donkey's back were some bottles of oil and wine. The Samaritan got them and rubbed some on the man's wounds as gently as he could. Then he bound them up with strips of clean cloth.

"Do you feel better now?" he asked the man. "Can you walk to my donkey if I help you? You shall ride him, and I will hold you on as I walk beside you."

The wounded man managed to get on the donkey's back. He was happy again. He kept looking in wonder at the Samaritan. How wonderful to know there was such kindness in the world!

They came to a roadside inn. The Samaritan
called to the innkeeper.

"Have you a good room for this poor fellow?
And have you any clothes?"

He put the man to bed and looked after him. In
the morning the wounded traveler felt much better.
The Samaritan went to the inn keeper.

14

"I cannot stay longer," he said, "or I would see to this man. Here is some money. Take care of him till he is better and can go home."

"If you have to spend more than I have given you, I will repay you when I come back this way again," said the Samaritan.

"Now," said Jesus, "who can tell me which of the three travelers—the priest, the Levite, or the Samaritan—was a kind and good neighbor to the man who fell among thieves?"

I shall not tell you the answer. I am sure you know it yourself, and you will always be a kind and good neighbor to anyone in trouble.

The Boy Who Left Home

"Jesus has some strange friends," the people sometimes said to one another. "He does not always go with good men and women, as surely a good man should."

Jesus heard what they said. He was sad. Didn't the people know that God had love even for sinners and was grieved to know that they had wandered far away from the kingdom of heaven, far away from God's love? Didn't they see that He too must love sinners and go to try and bring them back to God again?

"I will tell them another story," thought Jesus.

"There shall be three people in my story—a good son, a bad son, and a father who loves them both." And so he told the listening crowd this story.

There was once a rich man who had two sons. One day the younger son went to his father.

"Father," he said, "give me my share of the money, and I will go to the city and live there."

The father was sad. He gave his younger son his share of the money and said goodbye to him.

The younger son was pleased. He set off, thinking of all the money he had with him. What a fine time he would have!

He came to the town and looked for lodgings. As soon as the people saw that he had plenty of money they came around him. Ah, this was a fine life—he could give parties every day if he wanted to, and he could eat and drink from morning to night.

19

But money does not last forever. One day the boy found that he had none left—and when his money went, his fine friends melted away too.

"I must get some work," he thought. "I shall starve if I do not earn money to buy food."

But it was hard to get work. He had always been idle, and he did not know how to work hard. To make things worse, a great famine came to that land, and there was very little food.

At last he found a task. "You can look after my herd of pigs," said a farmer. So the boy sat under a tree, watching the grunting, greedy pigs. "I am so hungry that I could eat the empty pods that are thrown to these pigs," he thought.

"How foolish I have been! Why, in my father's house even the very lowliest servant gets enough bread to eat—and here I am envying the pigs their husks!"

He sat and thought of his father's house. He remembered the great kindness his father had always shown him.

"I shall go home!" he said to himself. "I will go to my father, and I will say to him: "Father, I have done wrong in God's sight and in yours too, and I am no longer worthy to be called your son. Make me one of your servants, and I will work hard for you."

He walked many many miles to get back to his home. He was dirty and his clothes were in rags.

But his father had not forgotten him. Each day he thought of him and prayed for him. Often he climbed up to the flat roof of his house just to see if by any chance his boy was coming home.

And then one day he saw someone in the distance who reminded him of his son. But no, surely this poor, ragged, miserable youth was not his beloved son?

"It is my son," said the old man at last, and he ran with great joy to meet him. All the way he ran, and took him in his arms and kissed him.

"Father!" said the son. "I have done wrong in God's sight and in yours, and I am no longer worthy to be called your son."

The old man did not let him say any more. He called to his servants.

"Get the best clothes we have in the house, and put them on my son," he said. "Get a ring for his finger too, and shoes for his feet. We will have a great feast tonight, so fetch the calf that is being fattened, and kill it for our supper. We will eat and be merry, for this son of mine I thought was dead is alive again; he was lost, but now he is found."

The youth was almost in tears. Everyone welcomed him; everyone was kind to him. How could he ever have been so foolish as to leave his home and family?

But wait—there was one person who was not pleased to see him back. The elder son was angry to hear that his younger brother had come home again and was being feasted and welcomed. He would not go to the feast.

He spoke angrily to his father. "Have I not worked for you all these years and obeyed you in everything?" he asked. "But you did not give me a feast!"

"Son, you have been always with me, sharing in all the good things I can give you," said the father gently. "You have lacked for nothing. It is right that we should welcome your brother and rejoice. We thought him dead, but he is alive; he was lost, but now he is found. We must make merry and be glad!"